Stanley Rule Level Co.

Stanley Improved Labor Saving Carpenters' Tools

Stanley Rule Level Co.

Stanley Improved Labor Saving Carpenters' Tools

ISBN/EAN: 9783337311407

Printed in Europe, USA, Canada, Australia, Japan

Cover: Foto ©Andreas Hilbeck / pixelio.de

More available books at **www.hansebooks.com**

STANLEY

Improved Labor Saving
Carpenters' Tools

Including
"BAILEY" ADJUSTABLE PLANE

STANLEY RULE & LEVEL CO.
New Britain, Conn., U.S.A.
SOLE MANUFACTURERS.

Plumbs and Levels

WITH GROUND GLASSES.

We offer these Levels as the highest type of Level which has ever been placed before a mechanic. The increased demand for a Level of the highest grade originally induced us to manufacture this line, and their sale has far exceeded our expectations.

Each.

No. 60. Mahogany Plumb and Level, Square Top Plate, Two Brass Lipped Side Views, with Ground Glasses, 24 to 30 inch.............................$2 90

No. 90. Mahogany Plumb and Level, Square Top Plate, Two Brass Lipped Side Views, Tipped, with Ground Glasses, 24 to 30 inches.............. 3 25

No. 95. Brass Bound, Mahogany Plumb and Level, Two Brass Lipped Side Views, with Ground Glasses, 24 to 30 inch........................... 6 00

No. 96. Brass Bound, Rosewood Plumb and Level, Two Brass Lipped Side Views, with Ground Glasses, 24 to 30 inch........................... 6 65

No. 98.

No. 98. Brass Bound, Rosewood Plumb and Level, Two Brass Lipped Side Views, with Ground Glasses,

Length,	6	9	12	18 inch.
Each,	$2 15	2 65	3 15	4 15

Metallic Plumbs and Levels.

No. 37.

No. 36. Japanned, Nickel-plated Trimmings, with Proved Glasses, Two Plumbs.

Length,	6	9	12	18	24	inch.
Each,	$1 00	1 25	1 50	1 75	2 00	

No. 37. Nickel-plated, with Ground Glasses and Eclipse Cases, Two Plumbs.

Length,	6	9	12	18	24	inch.
Each,	$2 00	2 50	3 00	3 50	4 00	

☞ Either of above will be furnished with groove cut in bottom (for working straight, etc.) if ordered, without extra charge.

"BED ROCK" Planes.

A NEW STYLE OF IRON BENCH PLANE.

The perfected design of this Plane allows a combination of the utmost solidity, with more adjustments than any Bench Plane ever produced.

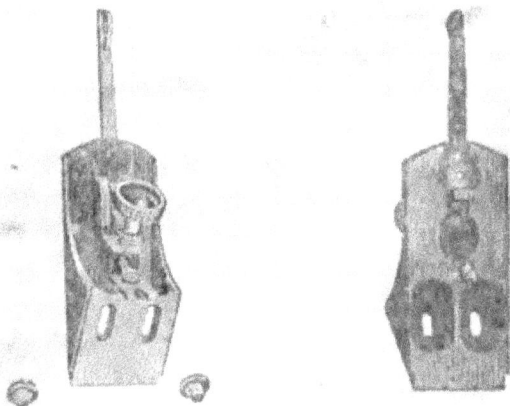

Both surfaces of the Frog are machined, and the bottom surface is in contact with the machined surface of the Plane body, thus giving the Cutting Iron as solid a bed as though resting on the Plane body itself.

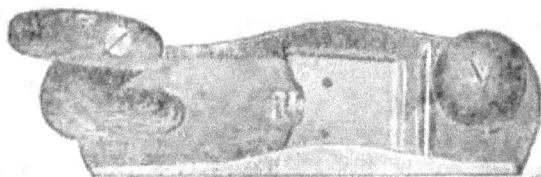

A Tongue is made on the bottom side of the Frog, and a corresponding groove is formed in the Plane body, overcoming any possibility of shifting or "wobbling" of the Frog.

"BED ROCK" Planes.

When it is desired to open or close the mouth, it can be easily done by turning the screw shown at the back of the Frog. The Tongue and groove mentioned insures that the Frog moves at a true right angle with the mouth.

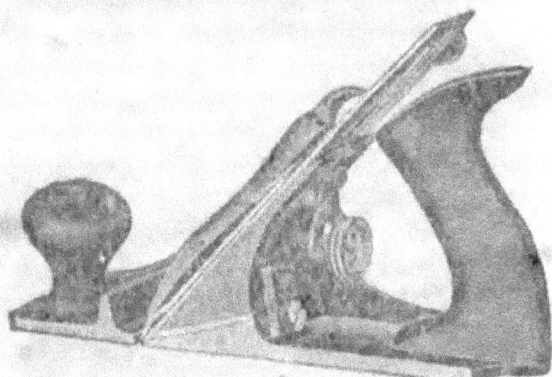

These new features will commend themselves to all who use Planes.

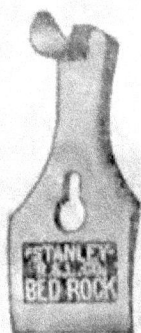

Ask your dealer to show you one of these tools, which you will know by the Cap.

"BED ROCK" Planes.

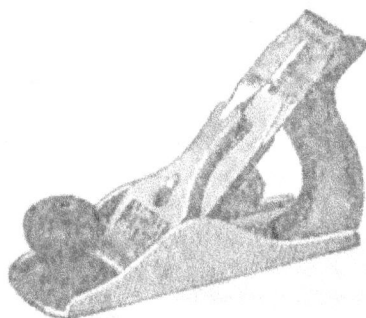

NO.			EACH
602	Smooth,	7 inches in Length, 1⅝ inch Cutter	$2 15
603	Smooth,	8 inches in Length, 1¾ inch Cutter	2 30
604	Smooth,	9 inches in Length, 2 inch Cutter	2 50
604½	Smooth,	10 inches in Length, 2⅜ inch Cutter	2 80

NO.			EACH
605	Jack,	14 inches in Length, 2 inch Cutter	$2 90
605½	Jack,	15 inches in Length, 2¼ inch Cutter	3 25
606	Fore,	18 inches in Length, 2⅜ inch Cutter	3 50
607	Jointer,	22 inches in Length, 2⅜ inch Cutter	4 20
608	Jointer,	24 inches in Length, 2⅝ inch Cutter	5 00

The Bed Rock Planes, with CORRUGATED BOTTOMS, will be furnished without additional expense, if so ordered.

Just a word about your orders.

Always give your dealer the *number* of the Plane you select. If you prefer a corrugated bottom it is only necessary to put the letter C after the number, as 604C, and he will know exactly what you want.

Bailey Adjustable Planes.

Manufactured only by the STANLEY RULE AND LEVEL COMPANY.

Iron Planes.

			Each.
No. 1.	Smooth, 5½ inches in Length,	1¼ inch Cutter,	$1 50
No. 2.	Smooth, 7 inches in Length,	1⅝ inch Cutter,	1 85
No. 3.	Smooth, 8 inches in Length,	1¾ inch Cutter,	2 00
No. 4.	Smooth, 9 inches in Length,	2 inch Cutter,	2 20
No. 4½.	Smooth, 10 inches in Length,	2⅜ inch Cutter,	2 50

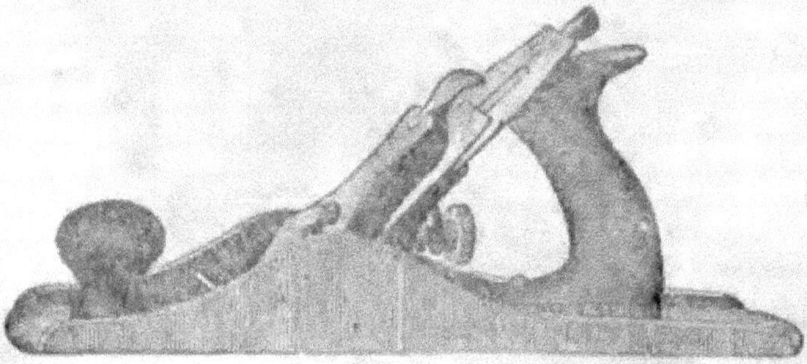

No. 5.	Jack, 14 inches in Length,	2 inch Cutter,	$2 50
No. 5½.	Jack, 15 inches in Length,	2¼ inch Cutter,	2 85
No. 6.	Fore, 18 inches in Length,	2⅜ inch Cutter,	3 20
No. 7.	Jointer, 22 inches in Length,	2⅜ inch Cutter,	3 65
No. 8.	Jointer, 24 inches in Length,	2⅝ inch Cutter,	4 35

☞ Planes Nos. 2, 3, 4, 4½, 5, 5½, 6, 7 and 8, with CORRUGATED BOTTOMS, will be furnished without additional expense, if so ordered.

Bailey Wood Planes.

				Each.
No. 21.	Smooth, 7	inches in Length, 1¾	in. Cutter....	$1 35
No. 22.	Smooth, 8	inches in Length, 1¾	in. Cutter....	1 35
No. 23.	Smooth, 9	inches in Length, 1¾	in. Cutter....	1 35
No. 24.	Smooth, 8	inches in Length, 2	in. Cutter....	1 35
No. 25.	Block, 9½	inches in Length, 1¾	in. Cutter....	1 35

No. 35.	Handle Smooth,	9 in. Length, 2	in. Cutter....	$1 70
No. 36.	Handle Smooth,	10 in. Length, 2⅜	in. Cutter....	1 85
No. 37.	Jenny Smooth,	13 in. Length, 2⅝	in. Cutter....	2 00

No. 26.	Jack,	15 inches in Length, 2	in. Cutter....	$1 50
No 27.	Jack,	15 inches in Length, 2⅛	in. Cutter....	1 70
No. 27½.	Jack,	15 inches in Length, 2¼	in. Cutter....	1 70
No. 28.	Fore,	18 inches in Length, 2⅜	in. Cutter....	1 85
No. 29.	Fore,	20 inches in Length, 2⅜	in. Cutter....	1 85
No. 30.	Jointer,	22 inches in Length, 2⅜	in. Cutter....	2 00
No. 31.	Jointer,	24 inches in Length, 2⅜	in. Cutter....	2 00
No. 32.	Jointer,	26 inches in Length, 2⅝	in. Cutter....	2 20
No. 33.	Jointer,	28 inches in Length, 2⅝	in. Cutter....	2 20
No. 34.	Jointer,	30 inches in Length, 2⅝	in. Cutter....	2 35

☞ Extra plane-woods can be supplied cheaply.

Bailey Adjustable Block Planes.

WITH IMPROVED THROAT ADJUSTMENT.

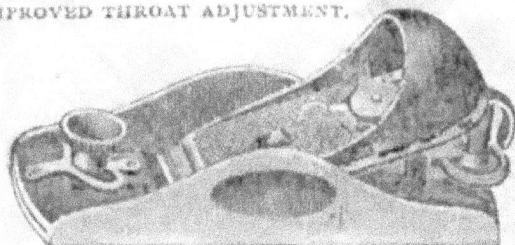

		Each.
No. 9½.	Block Plane, 6 inch Length, 1⅜ in. Cutter.....	$1 00
No. 9¾.	Rosewood Handle, 6 inches, 1⅜ in. Cutter......	1 20
No. 15.	Block Plane, 7 inch Length, 1⅝ in. Cutter......	1 10
No. 15½.	Rosewood Handle, 7 inches, 1⅝ in. Cutter......	1 30
No. 16.	Nickel Trimmings, 6 in. Length, 1⅜ in. Cutter,	1 15
No. 17.	Nickel Trimmings, 7 in. Length, 1⅝ in. Cutter,	1 25

Knuckle Joint Block Planes.

WITH IMPROVED   THROAT ADJUSTMENT.

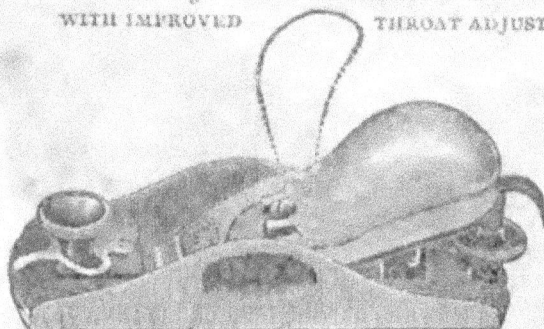

The knuckle-joint in the cap makes it a lever, too ; and placing
the cap in position will also clamp the cutter securely in its seat.

		Each.
No. 18.	Nickel Trimmings, 6 in. Length, 1⅜ in. Cutter,	$1 20
No. 19.	Nickel Trimmings, 7 in. Length, 1⅝ in. Cutter,	1 30

Low Angle Block Planes.

WITH IMPROVED THROAT ADJUSTMENT.

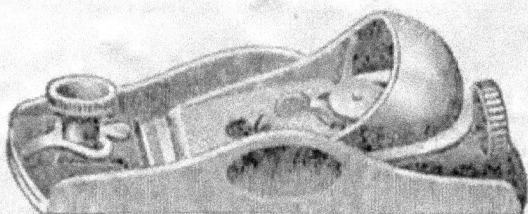

No. 60½.	Low-Angle, Block, 6 in. Length, 1⅛ in. Cutter,	$1 00
No. 65½.	Low-Angle, Block, 7 in. Length, 1⅝ in. Cutter,	1 10
No. 60.	Nickel Trimmings, 6 in. Length, 1⅛ in. Cutter,	1 15
No. 65.	Nickel Trimmings, 7 in. Length, 1⅝ in. Cutter,	1 25
	CAST STEEL CUTTERS for above Block Planes	17

Stanley Iron Block Planes.

Each.

No. 101.* Block Plane. 3½ inches in. Length, 1 in. Cutter, $0 15
No. 100. Block Plane, Handled, 3½ in. L'gth, 1 in. Cutter, 20

No. 102. Block Plane, 5½ inches in Length, 1¾ in. Cutter, 30
No. 103. Block Plane, Adjustable, 5½ inch, 1¾ in. Cutter, 45
       CAST STEEL CUTTERS for above Block Planes, 10

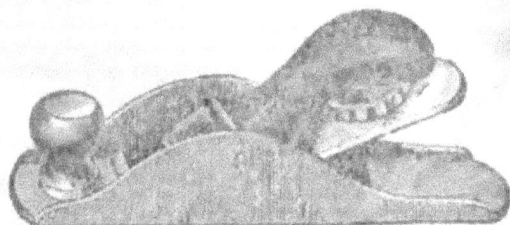

No. 110. Block Plane, 7½ inches in Length, 1¾ in. Cutter, 45
No. 120. Block Plane, Adjustable, 7½ inch, 1¾ in. Cutter, 60

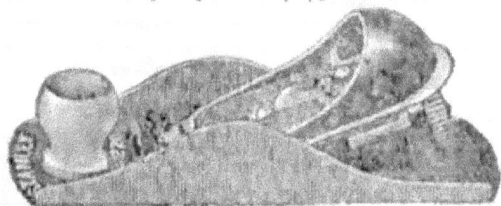

No. 220. Block Plane, Adjustable, 7½ inch. 1¾ in. Cutter, 60

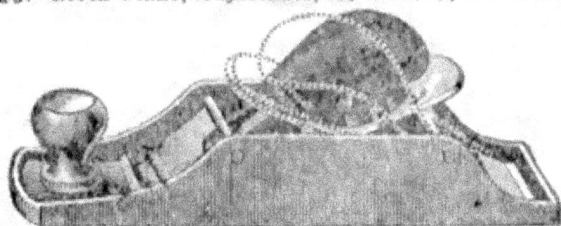

No. 130. Block Plane (Double-Ender), 8 in., 1¾ in. Cutter, 60
  This Plane has two slots and two cutter seats. By reversing
the position of the cutter and the clamping wedge, it can be
used close up into corners, or other difficult places.
       CAST STEEL CUTTERS, for above Block Planes.......... 17

Parts of Bailey Planes.

No.		No.	
1	Plane Iron.	10	Frog Screw.
2	Plane Iron Cap.	11	Handle.
3	Plane Iron Screw.	12	Knob.
4	Cap.	13	Handle "Bolt and Nut."
5	Cap Screw.	14	Knob "Bolt and Nut."
6	Frog.	15	Handle Screw.
7	"Y" Adjustment.	16	Bottom (Iron Plane.)
8	Brass Adjusting Nut	35	Top Casting (Wood Plane.)
9	Lateral Adjustment.	36	Bottom (Wood Plane.)

Parts of Block Planes.

No.		No.	
1B	Plane Iron	16B	Bottom (Adjust'ble Throat)
4B	Cap	20B	Mouth Piece.
5B	Cap Screw.	21B	Eccentric Plate.
7B	Adjusting Leve	22B	Knob.
8B	Adjusting Nut.	25B	Adjustable Frog.
9B	Lateral Adjustment.	28B	Adjusting Screw.
	46B	Bottom.	

The numbers in above list refer to the cut on opposite page.

In ordering parts for any Plane, give the number and name as given in the list and also the number of the Plane for which the parts are required.

The collection of parts marked A consists of the No. 6 Frog, No. 7 "Y" Adjustment, No. 8 Brass Adjusting Nut and No. 9 Lateral Adjustment. These parts we term "Frog Complete" and if a "Frog Complete" is ordered, the parts are always put together before shipment from our factory.

Many of our Special Planes, i. e., No. 113 Circular and No. 12 Scraper, etc., have some of the same parts as the Regular Line of Bailey Planes, and this list therefore, in many cases, will apply for ordering parts for Special Planes.

Prices of Plane Irons.

	1¼	1⅜	1¾	2	2⅛	2¼	2⅜	2⅝
Single Irons,	$0.18	.21	.23	.25	.27	.28	.29	.32 each.
Double Irons,	.32	.35	.38	.42	.45	.47	.48	.50

Orders for Plane Irons should designate number of the Plane for which they are wanted.

Parts of Bailey Planes.

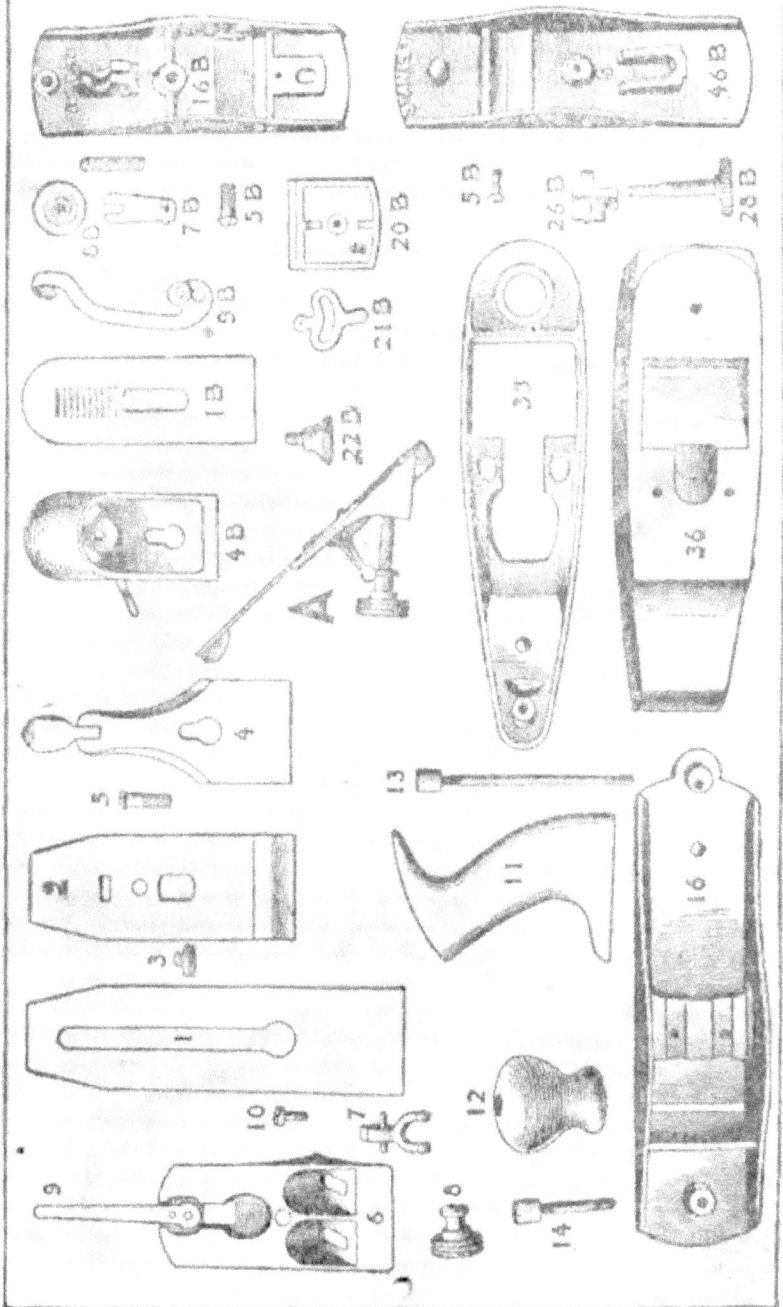

Stanley Adjustable Circular Plane.

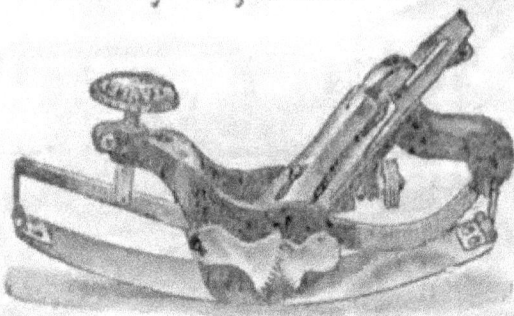

This Plane has a flexible steel face, which can be easily shaped to any required arc, either concave or convex, by turning the Knob on the front of the Plane.

Each.

No. 113. Adjustable Circular, 1¾ inch Cutter.......... $2 75

Improved Victor Circular Plane.

The Flexible Steel Face of this Plane can be made concave, or convex, by turning the screw which is attached to its center.

No. 20½. Adjustable Circular Plane, 1¾ inch Cutter, $3 15
No. 20. Circular Plane, Nickel-plated, 1¾ inch Cutter, 3 75

Stanley Cornering Tool.

For Pattern Makers, and used by all Wood-Workers in rounding sharp edges. The Tool is made in two numbers, with a different size Cutter at each end, so sharpened that owner can always cut with the grain without changing position of the work.

It requires no depth gauge, as the form of the tool allows it to cut only to a certain depth.

Each.

No. 28. 1-16 and ⅛ inches each, Flat Steel.............. $0 40
No. 29. ¼ and ⅜ inches each, Flat Steel.............. 40

Stanley Carriage Makers' Rabbet Plane.

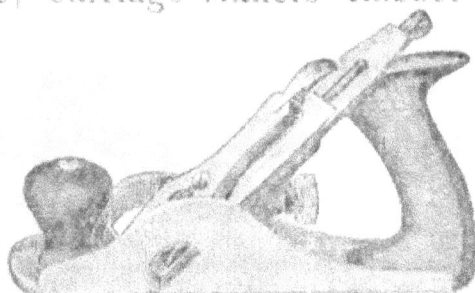

Each.

No. 10½. Carriage Makers' Rabbet, 9 in., 2¼ in. Cutter, $2 50
No. 10. Carriage Makers' Rabbet, 13 in., 2¼ in. Cutter, 3.00
With Corrugated Bottoms if so ordered, at same price.

Stanley Improved Scrub Plane.

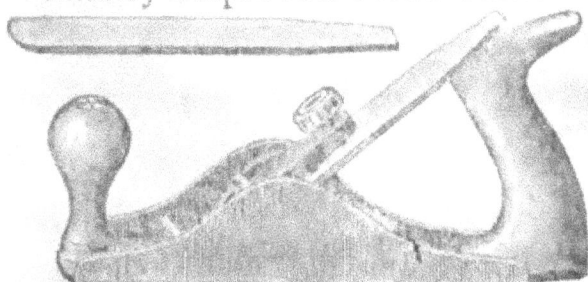

This Tool has a single Iron, with the cutting edge rounded.
It is particularly adapted for roughing down work before using
a Jack or other Plane. Each.

No. 40. Iron Stock, 9½ inches in Length, 1½ in. Cutter, $1 00
No. 40½. Iron Stock, 10½ inches in Length, 1½ in. Cutter, 1 35

Adjustable Scraper Plane.

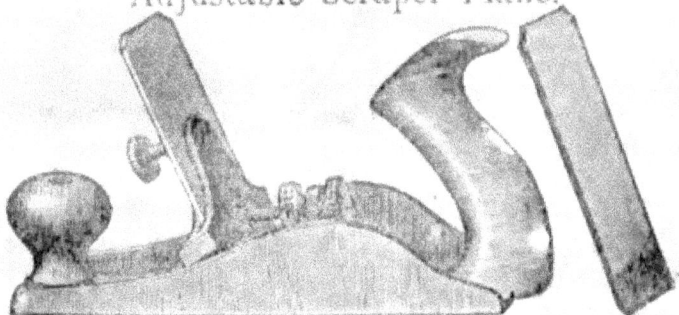

This Tool is used for scraping and finishing Veneers or Cabinet
work. It can be used equally well as a Tooth Plane.; and will
do excellent work in scraping off old paint and glue. Each.

No. 112. Adjustable Scraper, 9 in., 3 in. Cutter......... $2 00
CUTTERS, for Veneer Scraping............ 20
CUTTERS, for Toothing, Nos. 22, 28, 32 (22, 28 or 32 teeth per in.) 30

Improved Rabbet Plane.

This Plane will lie perfectly flat on either side and can be
used with right or left hand equally well, while planing into
corners or up against perpendicular surfaces.   Each.

No. 180.	Iron Stock, 8 in. Length, 1¼ in. wide.............	$1 00
No. 181.	Iron Stock, 8 in. Length, 1¼ in. wide.............	1 00
No. 182.	Iron Stock, 8 in. Length, 1 in. wide.............	1 00
No. 190.	Iron Stock, 8 in. Length, 1¼ in. wide, with spur,	1 15
No. 191.	Iron Stock, 8 in. Length, 1¼ in. wide, with spur,	1 15
No. 192.	Iron Stock, 8 in. Length, 1 in. wide, with spur,	1 15

Duplex Rabbet Plane and Filletster.

Remove the arm to which the fence is secured, and a Handled
Rabbet Plane is had, and with two seats for the Cutter, so that
the tool can be used as a Bull-Nose Rabbet if required.

The arm can be screwed into either side of the stock, mak-
ing a superior right or left hand Filletster.   Each.

No. 78. Iron Stock and Fence, 8½ in. Length, 1½ in. Cutter 1 50

Stanley Side Rabbet Plane.

A convenient Tool for side-
rabbeting and trimming
dados, mouldings & grooves
of all sorts. A reversible
nose-piece will give the tool
a form by which it will
work close up into corners
when required.

No. 98. Side Rabbet Plane, 4 inches, Right Hand....... $0 90
No. 99. Side Rabbet Plane, 4 inches, Left Hand........ 90

Stanley Adjustable Beading, Rabbet, and Matching Plane.

" " A Planing Mill within itself,"
says a Country Carpenter.

This Plane embraces (1) Beading and Center Beading Plane;
(2) Rabbet and Filletster; (3) Dado; (4) Plow; (5) Matching Plane;
(6) Sash Plane; and (7) a superior Slitting Plane.

Each Plane has seven Beading Tools (1-8, 3-16, 1-4, 5-16, 3-8, 7-16,
and 1-2 inch), ten Plow and Dado Bits (1-8, 3-16, 1-4, 5-16, 3-8, 7-16,
1-2, 5-8, 3-4 and 7-8 inch), a Slitting Blade, a Tonguing Tool and a
Sash Tool.

No. 45. Nickel-plated, with Twenty Tools, Bits, etc., each, $8 00

Plow Dado & Rabbet Tools.

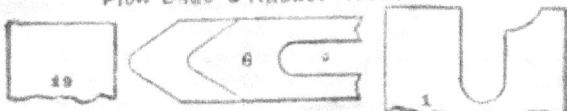

Slitting Tool.   Sash Tool

Beading Tools.   Match Tool

Hollows and Rounds, for Plane No. 45.

No.	6	8	10	12	
Cutter,	½	⅝	¾	1	Inch Wide.
Works,	¾	1	1¼	1½	Inch Circle.
Price,	$1 40	1 40	1 40	1 40	Per Pair.

Nosing Tool, for Plane No. 45.

No. 5. Nosing Tool, 1¼ in. (attach same as above), each, $1 00

Reeding Tools, for Plane No. 45.

Size of Beads, either 1-8, 3-16 or 1-4 inch—Uniform Price
2 Beads, .20.   3 Beads, .30,   4 Beads, .40,   5 Beads, .50   each.

Cutters for Universal Plane.

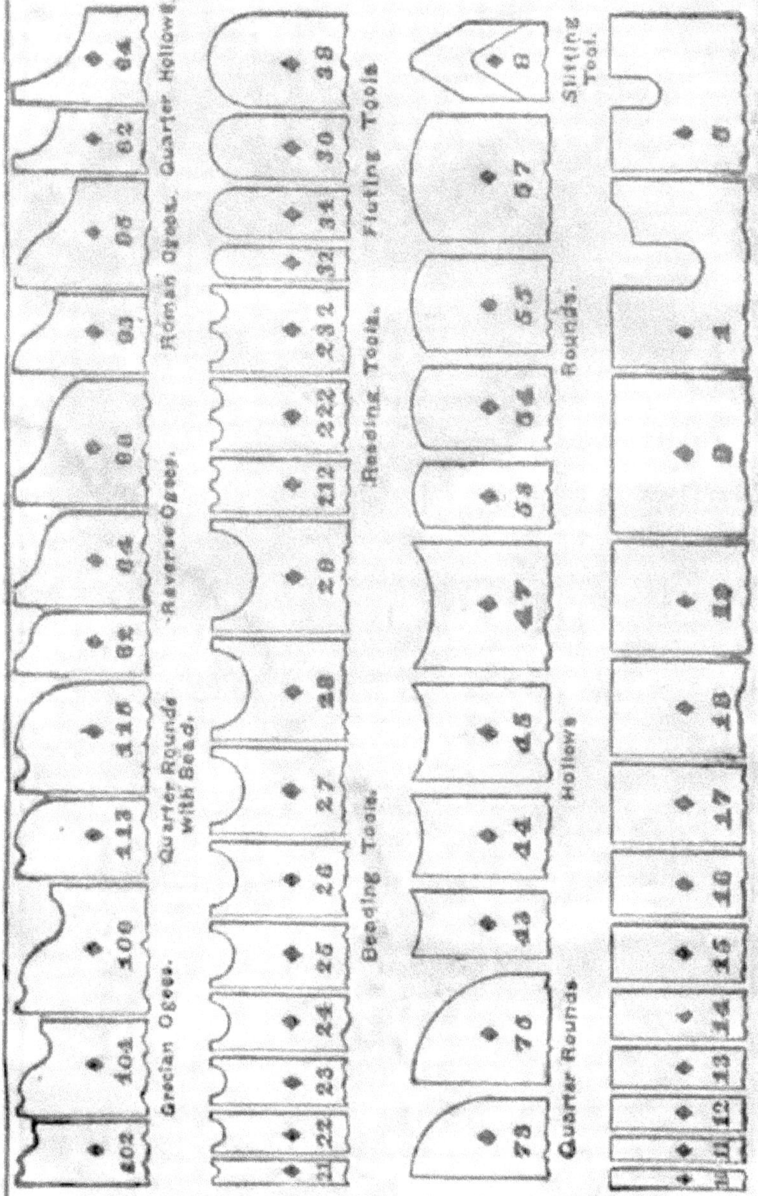

Quarter Hollows.

Roman Ogee. 64 62 65 63 60 64 62 115 113 100 104 102

Fluting Tools. 38 30 34 32

Reading Tools. 232 222 212 29 28 27 26 25 24 23 22 21

Sliting Tool. 6

Rounds. 67 55 54 53 47 46 44 43

Quarter Rounds. 79 78

Match Tool. 5 4 3 2 10 18 17 16 15 14 13 12 11 10

Filleter.

"Sash Tool."

Plow, Dado & Rabbet Tools.

Grecian Ogee.

Reverse Ogee.

Quarter Rounds with Bead.

Beading Tools.

Hollows

Tools are shown one-half full size.

A Main Stock (A) with transverse sliding arms; a depth gauge (F) adjusted by a screw; and a Slitting Cutter with stop. A Sliding Section (B) with a vertically adjustable bottom. The Auxiliary Center Bottom (C) is to be placed in front of the Cutter, as an extra support, or stop, when needed.

Stanley Patent Universal Plane.

This Tool, in the hands of an ordinary carpenter, can be used for all lines of work covered by a full assortment of so-called Fancy Planes.

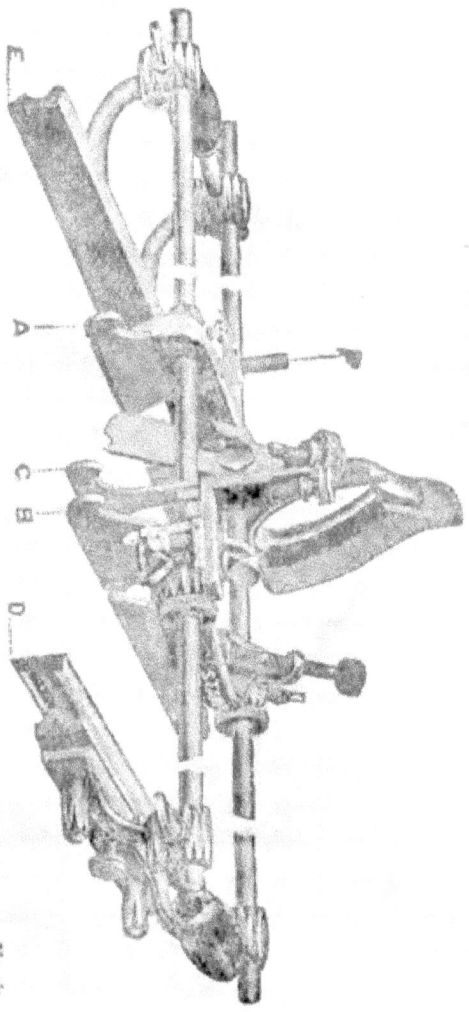

No. 55. Stanley's Universal Plane, 53 Tools, Bits, etc.................. $16 00 Each.

The Plane is nickel-plated; the 52 Cutters are arranged in four separate cases; and the entire outfit is packed in a neat Wooden Box.

Fence D has a lateral adjustment by means of a screw, for extra fine work. The Fences can be used on either side of the Plane, and the rosewood guides can be tilted to any desired angle, up to 45 degrees, by loosening screws on face. Fence H can be reversed for Center Beading wide boards, when necessary.

Improved Dado Planes.

The Cutter is set on a skew. Plane is fitted with a Depth Gauge, adjustable by means of a Thumb Screw. Also with two adjustable Spurs, which can be adjusted to take up wear as well as for depth of cut.

		Each.
No. 39.	Iron Stock, 8 inches long, ¼ in. Cutter	$1 50
No. 39.	Iron Stock, 8 inches long, ⅜ in. Cutter	1 50
No. 39.	Iron Stock, 8 inches long, ½ in. Cutter	1 50
No. 39.	Iron Stock, 8 inches long, ⅝ in. Cutter	1 50
No. 39.	Iron Stock, 8 inches long, ¾ in. Cutter	1 50
No. 39.	Iron Stock, 8 inches long, ⅞ in. Cutter	1 50
No. 39.	Iron Stock, 8 inches long, 1 in. Cutter	1 50
	CUTTERS for above Planes	20

In ordering, designate by No. 39 and width of Cutter.

Stanley Rabbet and Block Plane.

A detachable side will easily change this Tool from a Block Plane to a Rabbet Plane, or *vice versa*. The cutter is set on a *skew*.

		Each.
No. 140.	Rabbet and Block Plane, with detachable side, 7 inches in length, 1¾ in. Cutter	1 25

Adjustable Cabinet Makers' Rabbet Plane

This Plane is designed for fine Cabinet work where extreme accuracy is required. The sides and bottom being square with each other the Plane will lie perfectly flat on either side, and can be used right or left.

Both the cutter and width of throat opening are adjustable. The Plane is nickel-plated and fitted with the "Handy" feature.

No. 92.

		Each.
No. 90. Bull-Nose,	4 inches in Length, 1 in. Cutter,	$2 00
No. 92. Rabbet Plane, 5¼ inches in Length, ⅞ in. Cutter,	2 00
No. 93. Rabbet Plane, 6½ inches in Length, 1 in. Cutter,	2 35
No. 94. Rabbet Plane, 7½ inches in Length, 1¼ in. Cutter,	2 75
Cutters for above Planes..........................	30

Woodworkers' Router Plane.

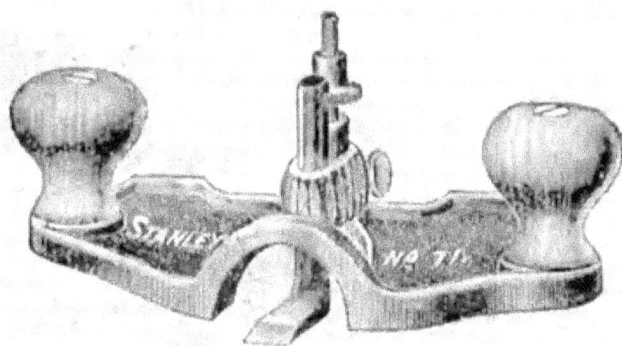

No. 71.	Nickel-plated Stock, with Steel Bits (¼ and ½ in.)	$1 85
No. 71½.	Closed Throat, with Steel Bits ¼ and ½ in.	1 50
	Cutters for above Planes, (¼ or ½ in.)	30

Stanley Universal Spoke Shave.

No. 67. Universal Spoke Shave, for curved or straight work. $1.50

Both Handles are detachable, and either of them can be screwed into a socket on top of the stock, thus enabling the owner to work into corners, or panels, as no other spoke shave can do.

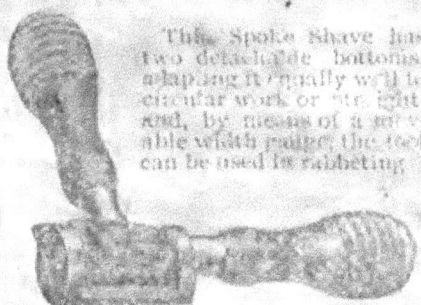

This Spoke Shave has two detachable bottoms, adapting it equally well to circular work or straight, and, by means of a movable mouth gauge, the tool can be used for rabbeting.

Stanley Improved Butt Gauge.

A Metallic Butt Gauge, having one bar with two steel cutters fixed upon it. When the cutter at the outer end of this bar is set for gauging on the edge of the door, the cutter at the inner end of the bar is already set for gauging from the back of the jamb. The other bar has a steel cutter to accurately gauge for the thickness of the butt.

The form of the Tool is convenient for carrying in the pocket. It is so constructed that the bars cannot fall out of the stock.

No. 95. Nickel-plated Butt Gauge............................$0.75

Improved Marking and Mortise Gauge.

No. 91.

This Gauge is made of metal, and has two graduated bars. The steel points are set very near the ends of the bars, to admit of being used close up into a rabbet, or corner.   Each

No. 90. Nickel-plated Marking Gauge.....................$0.35
No. 91. Nickel-plated Marking and Mortise Gauge....... .65

.

www.ingramcontent.com/pod-product-compliance
Lightning Source LLC
Chambersburg PA
CBHW021611270326
41931CB00009B/1429